SOCIAL PROTECTION IN INDIA

A COMPREHENSIVE GUIDE

SUBHASH CHAUDHARY

Made with ♥ on the Notion Press Platform
www.notionpress.com

This book is dedicated to all those who strive to improve the lives and welfare of marginalized and vulnerable populations around the world.

We owe a debt of gratitude to the countless people in the social protection sector, from government officials to service providers, who work hard to ensure that everyone has access to the basic needs and rights that they deserve.

We also extend our appreciation to those who have gone before us, who have paved the way for us to continue to build on their legacy.

Thank you for your dedication, your commitment and your passion for making a positive difference in the world.

We hope this book provides useful guidance and insight into the world of social protection, and that it helps to improve the lives of those who need it the most.

Contents

Foreword

The concept of social protection is becoming increasingly important in today's world. As the global population grows, so does the need for protection in the face of poverty, unemployment, and other social risks. This book is designed to provide a comprehensive guide to social protection, from the basics to the most advanced concepts.

This book is written in a clear and concise manner, making it accessible to everyone from the beginner to the advanced student. It covers the history of social protection, the different types of social protection programs available, and the strategies for designing and implementing successful social protection policies. It also delves into the economics of social protection, the legal and ethical considerations, and the challenges of implementation.

The goal of this book is to provide an overview of the field of social protection, as well as an in-depth exploration of its various facets. By understanding social protection, we can make informed decisions about how to address poverty and other social risks.

This book is meant to be a valuable resource for anyone interested in social protection, whether they are a policymaker, a student, or a concerned citizen. I hope that this book will be a useful tool in helping to create a more equitable and secure world for all.

Sincerely,
Subhash Chaudhary

Preface

Social Protection is an important part of any society. It provides individuals and families with the means to adjust to changing economic and social conditions. This book provides a comprehensive guide to understanding and implementing social protection policies and programs.

This book is intended to be an authoritative and comprehensive guide to social protection for both practitioners and policy makers. It provides an overview of the history of social protection and its theoretical and practical foundations.

It also covers topics such as social assistance, pensions, labor market protection, health insurance, and other social protection programs.

The book draws on the experience and knowledge of experts from around the world.

It provides an in-depth analysis of the challenges and opportunities of social protection, and offers practical advice on how to implement effective social protection policies and programs.

The book is divided into four main sections. The first section provides an overview of the history and theory of social protection.

The second section discusses the various components of social protection, including social assistance, pensions, labor market protection, health insurance, and other social protection programs.

The third section examines the challenges and opportunities of social protection, and the fourth section offers practical advice on how to implement effective social protection policies and programs.

This book is a must-read for anyone interested in learning about social protection and its implementation. It is an invaluable resource for policymakers, practitioners, and academics alike.

Acknowledgements

I thank my editor, Uttam Kumar, for his immense help in creating this book. His guidance and insight were invaluable in making this book a reality.

I would also like to thank my family and friends for their support throughout this project. Their encouragement and belief in me motivated me to keep working on this book.

I owe a great debt of gratitude to the many experts who were kind enough to share their knowledge and experience with me. Without their expertise, this book would not be possible.

Finally, I thank the readers and reviewers who have given me feedback on this book. Your comments have been invaluable in helping me to improve and refine it. Thank you all for your support.

Prologue

The concept of social protection has come to the fore in the 21st century, with nations the world over seeking to provide a safety net for their citizens in the face of economic and social insecurity.

Social protection is a broad and complex subject, touching on a number of areas including health, education, pensions, employment, and other services.

This book provides a comprehensive guide to social protection, exploring its history, present state, and future potential.

It examines the various forms of social protection and their implications for individuals, communities, and governments.

It also looks at the challenges of implementing social protection and the strategies that can be adopted to ensure its effectiveness.

This book is aimed at a wide audience, from those looking to understand the basics of social protection to those seeking more in-depth information.

It is written in an accessible style and is intended to be used as a reference tool for those wanting to learn more about this important area of public policy.

We hope that this book will serve as a useful source of information and inspiration for anyone seeking to better understand the world of social protection.

CHAPTER ONE

The History and Evolution of Social Protection

Social protection has been around for centuries, but its modern conception began in the late 19th century. Initially, social protection was limited to only providing basic needs such as food, shelter, and clothing to the most vulnerable members of society.

Over time, however, social protection has evolved to become a comprehensive system of policies and programs aimed at reducing poverty and social exclusion.

In the early 20th century, the concept of social protection was further developed, as governments began to recognize the need for a more comprehensive approach to providing social security and protection.

This led to the introduction of a variety of policies and programs, such as unemployment insurance, health insurance, and social assistance. In the decades that followed, the scope of social protection continued to expand.

In the United States, the Social Security Act of 1935 established the modern social security system, which provided a range of benefits to retirees and the disabled.

In Europe, the post-World War II period saw the emergence of a comprehensive social security system, which provided a range of benefits such as pensions and unemployment insurance.

In recent decades, the scope of social protection has grown even further. Governments have increasingly recognized the need to address poverty and social exclusion more comprehensively.

As a result, a range of new policies and programs have been introduced, such as social assistance, employment insurance, disability insurance, and family allowance programs.

At the same time, governments have also increased their focus on preventive measures, such as education, health care, and employment programs.

This shift has been driven by a recognition of the need to address the underlying causes of poverty and social exclusion, rather than simply providing temporary relief.

Today, social protection is an integral part of the social welfare system in most countries around the world. It is seen as an essential tool for promoting economic and social development, reducing inequality, and ensuring that all members of society have access to basic needs and opportunities.

Social protection is also seen as an important way of promoting social cohesion, as it provides security and stability to those most vulnerable. In conclusion, social protection has come a long way since its inception in the late 19th century.

It has evolved from a basic system of providing basic needs to a comprehensive system of policies and programs that aim to reduce poverty and social exclusion.

As governments continue to recognize the importance of social protection, it is likely that the scope and complexity of social protection will continue to expand in the years ahead.

CHAPTER TWO

The Components of Social Protection

Social protection in India is composed of four main components: health systems, social security, poverty alleviation, and labour market regulations.

This chapter outlines the key components and their respective roles in providing social protection in India.

1. Health Systems: Health systems are the cornerstone of social protection in India. They are designed to provide access to quality healthcare services for all citizens, regardless of their economic status. The government provides a variety of public health services, such as primary healthcare, preventive care, and emergency services. The government also subsidizes the cost of healthcare services, making them more affordable for the population. Health systems have been instrumental in reducing the burden of communicable diseases, improving maternal and child health, and providing access to medical care for those living in rural areas.

2. Social Security: The government of India provides social protection through a system of social security. This includes pensions, unemployment benefits, and disability benefits. Pension schemes provide a regular income to

retirees, while unemployment benefits provide financial support to those who have lost their job. Disability benefits provide financial assistance to those who are unable to work due to a disability. Social security is an important component of social protection and provides financial security for individuals and families.

3. Poverty Alleviation: Poverty alleviation is an important component of social protection in India. The government has implemented several programmes to reduce poverty, such as the Mahatma Gandhi National Rural Employment Guarantee Act (MGNREGA). This programme provides 100 days of employment to rural workers and guarantees a minimum wage. Other poverty alleviation programmes include the Pradhan Mantri Awaas Yojana, which provides housing for the poor, and the Rashtriya Swasthya Bima Yojana, which provides health insurance to the poor.

4. Labour Market Regulations: Labour market regulations are another important component of social protection in India. These regulations are designed to protect workers from exploitation and unfair treatment. The government has implemented laws such as the Minimum Wages Act, the Equal Remuneration Act, and the Maternity Benefit Act, which set out workers' rights and guaranteed fair wages and working conditions. Labour market regulations are essential for ensuring that workers are adequately protected.

These four components are essential for providing social protection in India. They provide access to healthcare, financial security, and fair working conditions. Social protection is essential for ensuring that all citizens have access to basic services and can lead dignified life.

CHAPTER THREE

The Implementation of Social Protection

Social protection in India is a complex system, with multiple layers of implementation and execution. This chapter will explore the implementation of social protection in India, and the various challenges associated with it.

The implementation of social protection in India is largely done through the public sector, with some private sector involvement.

The Government of India is the primary provider of social protection, through a variety of schemes. These schemes cover a wide range of topics, such as health, education, employment, income support, and social security.

The Government of India has established several Ministries and Departments to oversee the implementation of social protection in India.

These Ministries and Departments are responsible for formulating policies, developing programs, and monitoring the implementation of social protection initiatives.

The primary Ministry responsible for social protection in India is the Ministry of Labour and Employment.

This Ministry is responsible for providing income support and social security to vulnerable groups in India. It also oversees the implementation of schemes such as the National Social Security Scheme (NSSS) and the Mahatma Gandhi National Rural Employment Guarantee Scheme (MGNREGS).

In addition to the public sector, the private sector also plays an important role in the implementation of social protection in India.

Private sector companies, such as banks and insurance companies, provide a variety of services and products to help protect the vulnerable population.

These services and products can range from basic health insurance, to more complex financial instruments such as pension plans.

In addition to the public and private sectors, civil society organizations and non-governmental organizations (NGOs) also play an important role in the implementation of social protection in India.

These organizations often provide direct services to the vulnerable populations, such as microfinance, legal aid, and health and education services.

Despite the multitude of players involved in the implementation of social protection in India, there are still significant challenges associated with it.

These challenges include inadequate funding, lack of coordination between different stakeholders, and the lack of effective monitoring and evaluation systems.

To successfully implement social protection in India, it is important to ensure adequate resources are allocated, coordination between different stakeholders is improved, and effective monitoring and evaluation systems are in place.

It is also important to ensure that social protection initiatives are responsive to the needs of the vulnerable populations, and that they are tailored to meet the specific needs of each group.

These measures will help to ensure that social protection initiatives are successful, and that they are able to provide the necessary support to the most vulnerable populations in India.

CHAPTER FOUR

Case Studies of Social Protection

Social protection has become a critical component of development policies in India. This chapter will explore how India has implemented social protection programs using case studies from different states.

It will focus on the successes and challenges faced by the government and its citizens in implementing such programs. The National Food Security Act (NFSA) is one of the most significant social protection initiatives in India.

The NFSA provides food security to two-thirds of India's population and seeks to ensure that vulnerable populations have access to adequate nutrition. The Act has been implemented in several states, including Andhra Pradesh, Bihar, Gujarat, Karnataka, Maharashtra, Tamil Nadu, and Uttar Pradesh. In each of these states, the NFSA has had a positive impact on reducing poverty and hunger.

The Mahatma Gandhi National Rural Employment Guarantee Act (MGNREGA), launched in 2006, is another example of a successful social protection program in India. It guarantees 100 days of wage employment to every rural household in India. The program has been successful in providing livelihood opportunities to millions of poor households and reducing poverty in rural areas.

The Janani Suraksha Yojana (JSY) is a government program that provides financial incentives to pregnant women to ensure safe delivery and post-natal care. The program has been successful in reducing maternal mortality in India, particularly in rural and tribal areas.

The Pradhan Mantri Ujjwala Yojana (PMUY) is a program launched in 2016 to provide free LPG connections to women living in poverty. The program has been successful in providing clean and smoke-free cooking to millions of households. The Pradhan Mantri Awas Yojana (PMAY) is an urban housing scheme launched in 2015 to provide affordable housing to the urban poor. The scheme has been successful in providing housing to millions of urban poor households.

The Rashtriya Swasthya Bima Yojana (RSBY) is a health insurance scheme launched in 2008 to provide financial protection to the poor and vulnerable sections of the population. The scheme has been successful in providing health insurance to millions of households in India.

The Indira Gandhi National Old Age Pension Scheme (IGNOAPS) is a pension scheme launched in 2007 to provide a basic monthly pension to elderly people living in poverty. The scheme has been successful in providing financial security to the elderly population in India.

In conclusion, India has made significant progress in the implementation of social protection programs.

Each of the programs discussed in this chapter has positively impacted the lives of millions of people living in poverty.

The challenges faced in the implementation of social protection programs remain, however, and further efforts are needed to ensure that these programs reach the most vulnerable populations in India.

CHAPTER FIVE

The Future of Social Protection

Social protection is a vital part of India's development agenda, and the government has made considerable progress in recent years in improving the social protection system. However, there is still much to be done to ensure that all Indians have access to the social protection they need. This chapter will examine the future of social protection in India, focusing on the challenges and opportunities that lie ahead.

First, it is important to recognize the importance of social protection in India. Social protection can help reduce poverty, inequality, and vulnerability, while also contributing to economic growth. It can also help to ensure greater social cohesion and reduce social exclusion. As such, it is essential that the government continues to invest in social protection and ensure that it is accessible to all Indians.

Second, the government must continue to focus on improving the existing social protection system in India. This includes increasing the coverage of existing programs, such as the Mahatma Gandhi National Rural Employment Guarantee Act and the National Food Security Act, and ensuring that they are better-targeted to the needs of the population. Additionally, the government must continue to create new social protection programs to address the needs of the most vulnerable populations, such as women, children, and the elderly.

Third, technological innovation can be a powerful tool for improving social protection in India. Technology can help to increase access to social protection, reduce administrative costs, and improve data collection and analysis. For example, the government can use digital financial technologies, such as mobile banking, to make social protection programs more accessible to remote populations. Additionally, the government can use artificial intelligence and predictive analytics to better target social protection programs to those who need them most.

Finally, there is a need to improve the coordination and collaboration between the different stakeholders involved in social protection in India. This includes the government, civil society organizations, and the private sector. By working together, these actors can ensure that social protection is effective and efficient, and that it reaches those who need it most.

In conclusion, the future of social protection in India is bright. The government has made significant progress in recent years, but there is still much to be done. By continuing to invest in social protection and making use of technological innovations, the government can ensure that all Indians have access to the social protection they need.

CHAPTER SIX

The failure of Social Protection

In India, social protection has largely been ineffective in providing any meaningful protection or assistance to those in need. Despite the numerous government schemes and programmes aimed at providing social protection, the results have been largely inadequate.

This chapter will explore the reasons for the failure of social protection in India and the implications for the country's development. The biggest reason for the failure of social protection in India is the fact that the government has failed to provide sufficient resources for the schemes and programmes.

Though the government has allocated a substantial amount of resources for social protection, the fact remains that much of this money is diverted to other areas of the economy and to other government schemes. This has resulted in a lack of sufficient funding for social protection, thus leading to its failure.

Another reason for the failure of social protection in India is the lack of a comprehensive framework to guide the implementation of the schemes and programmes.

Many of the schemes and programmes are implemented in a haphazard manner, without any clear direction or plan. This has resulted in a lack of effective implementation of the programmes, thus leading to their failure.

The third reason for the failure of social protection in India is the lack of adequate coordination among various government departments and agencies.

There is a lack of clear communication between various government departments and agencies, which has resulted in a lack of coordination and effective implementation of the social protection schemes and programmes.

Finally, the fourth reason for the failure of social protection in India is the lack of public participation. Many of the social protection schemes and programmes require public participation in order to be effective.

However, due to a lack of awareness and a lack of incentive to participate, public participation in social protection programmes has been minimal.

The failure of social protection in India has had a number of implications for the country's development.

Firstly, it has resulted in a lack of access to basic services and resources for the most vulnerable sections of the population.

Secondly, it has led to a widening of the gap between the rich and the poor, as the benefits of social protection have largely been enjoyed by the affluent sections of the population.

Finally, it has created an environment of economic insecurity, as the lack of adequate social protection has made it difficult for individuals to plan for the future.

In conclusion, the failure of social protection in India has had a number of negative consequences for the country's development. It is therefore essential that the government takes steps to address the issues that have led to the failure of social protection in India and ensure that all citizens have access to adequate social protection.

CHAPTER SEVEN

Conclusion

In conclusion, Social Protection in India has come a long way since its inception in the late 19th century. From the traditional safety nets of the extended family and community to the modern welfare systems implemented by the government, India has made great strides in providing social protection for its citizens.

While there is still work to be done to better implement social protection schemes, overall, the country is making great strides.

By increasing its focus on social protection, India can ensure that its citizens are supported when they are in need, and can provide an example for other countries to emulate. In this way, Social Protection in India can create a brighter future for all its citizens.

Read More

Reference list:

1. Bhatia, A. (2009). Social Protection in India. New Delhi: Oxford University Press.

2. Gaiha, R. and Kulkarni, V. (2010). Social Protection in India: A Review. Economic and Political Weekly, 45(37), 39-45.

3. Gaiha, R., Kulkarni, V. and Unni, J. (2010). Social Protection in India: An Overview. Economic and Political Weekly, 45(37), 47-51.

4. Radhakrishna, R. (2011). Social Protection in India: Issues and Challenges. Delhi: Sage.

5. Das, P. (2012). Social Protection in India: A Study of the Targeted Public Distribution System. New Delhi: Sage.

6. Joshi, V. (2013). Social Protection in India: Trends and Challenges. Economic and Political Weekly, 48(31-33), 38-45.

7. Tiwari, D. (2014). Social Protection in India: An Overview. New Delhi: Oxford University Press.

www.ingramcontent.com/pod-product-compliance
Lightning Source LLC
Chambersburg PA
CBHW021330160726
47994CB00004B/1699